Passing It On

FOUR GENERATIONS OF GRAHAM TRADITIONS

My sisters Bunny, Anne and me after a day of swimming

Mother and Daddy 1960

Santa Claus with me

Mother holding newborn brother Ned with Franklin watching

My family together in Switzerland. Clockwise: Daddy, Ned, Mother, Anne, Me, Bunny & Franklin

Me being "big sister" to Bunny, Anne and Franklin

Passing It On

FOUR GENERATIONS OF GRAHAM TRADITIONS

GIGI TCHIVIDJIAN-GRAHAM

McCracken Press

NEW YORK - NEW ORLEANS

Passing It On

Published by McCracken Press™
An imprint of Multi Media Communicators, Inc.
575 Madison Avenue, NY 10022

Designed by Stephanie Schaffer, Laura Carr, and Samuel Chapin.
Cover photo by Russ Busby.

Unless otherwise indicated, all Scripture references are from The Holy Bible:
New International Version, © 1973, 1978, 1984 by the International Bible Society.
Used by permission of Zondervan Bible Publishers.

Scripture references marked NKJV are from The Bible:
The New King James Version, © 1984 by Thomas Nelson, Inc. Used by permission.

Scripture references marked TLB are from The Living Bible, © 1971 by
Tyndale House Publishers, Wheaton, IL. Used by permission.

Scripture references marked Phillips are from J.B. Phillips: The New Testament in Modern English, J.B. Phillips, ©
1958. Used by permission of Macmillan Publishing Co., Inc.

Scripture references marked Amplified are from The Amplified New Testament,
© 1954, 1958 by The Lockman Foundation. Used by permission.

It is with gratitude that the majority of the formal Graham family photographs were taken by our long-time friend and professional
photographer, Russ Busby. Photo on page 19 © Gold Photography. The photos on pages 29 and 78 by Jean Schlammer; the photos
on pages 60, 77 and 79 Maury Scobee; photo on page 85 by Mark Zier; photo on page 88 by Bryn Alan; photos on pages 94 and 95 by
Don Young. The photo of Bunny's family on page 63 © Charles Clemmer, Staunton, VA. Other photos come from the Graham-
Tchividjian family albums.

Library of Congress Catalog Card Number: 93-078599
ISBN 1-56977-500-1
10 9 8 7 6 5 4 3 2 1
First Edition
Printed in the United States

Front Cover:
Front—Mother, Stetson Tchividjian, Daddy and Antony. Standing left to right—David Barker, Hope Tchividjian
(in Berdjette's arms) Berdjette, me, Seth Barker (in my arms), Aram, Lydia, Basyle, Charlee Tchividjian, Lisa, Stephen Nelson. With a
family our size it is difficult to get everyone together; missing from the photo are my
husband Stephan, my son Tullian, and daughter Jerushah.

Back Cover:
Standing left to right—Anne, me. Sitting—Bunny, Mother, Ned, Daddy, Franklin.

ACKNOWLEDGEMENTS

This year is special. It is my parents' 50th wedding anniversary and my father's 75th birthday.

To all who have put in long hours of hard work and creative energy making this book a reality in time for my parents' 50th wedding anniversary, I am deeply grateful.

To Jack Bennett, Dick Ohman, Doug Holladay, Dean Overman and Jarrell McCracken, who believed in me and in this project. To Larry Libby and Bill Griffin who patiently edited the manuscript.

To Ron Friedman and Laura Carr, two of the most creative people that I have been privileged to work with, who literally worked around the clock, and still remained pleasant.

To my family for putting up with a stressed out mom so that I could meet deadlines.

To my husband Stephan for his encouragement and belief in me and in this project.

But, especially to my best friend and sister Bunny, who believed so much in this book, that she introduced me to Multi Media Communicators and then spent many hours cutting, pasting, going through photographs, making countless calls, etc., to help me complete this task. I simply say...

thank you and I love you.

Mother and Daddy's
wedding day
August 13, 1943

DEDICATION

With deep gratitude, this book is dedicated to all the godly men and women who have been part of my spiritual heritage, and who have been faithful in "passing it on."

To "Bomb" my maternal great-grandmother (the only great-grandparent that I knew), to my grandparents Lao I and Lao Niang, and to Mother and Daddy Graham. To Mother and Daddy, who provided both the atmosphere and the examples that made me want to pass on what I had received, and to my husband Stephan, who asked me to share his heritage and provides the love and leadership that make it a joy to continue passing our heritage on to our own children and grandchildren.

But, especially to my seven children, their spouses, my grandchildren, and my twelve nieces and nephews… pass it on.

Oh, that their hearts would be inclined to fear me and keep all my commands always, so that it might go well with them and their children forever.

(Deuteronomy 5: 29)

An early family photograph

Table of Contents

Me with my Great Dane, Princess

Gigi

Gigi is the first of our five children—mother of seven of our nineteen grandchildren and grandmother of our four great-grandchildren. It seems but yesterday that she was home—the stubborn, quick-tempered, sensitive, honest, lovable little manager of her brothers and sisters. "Everyone," her mother once laughed, "ought to have at least one Gigi." She was a terror, believe it or not. Once, her mother came home, and the maid, Beatrice, met her at the door. "Mrs. Graham, I don't know what is getting into the children, but they went up to the neighbor's house and sassed her." Well, this comes under moral issues, so her mother went up the stairs with switch in hand. Gigi saw her coming and being the eldest and spokesman for the group said, "Mother, you can't blame us. It wasn't our fault. It was the devil! He's the one that got into us and made us do it, so you can't blame us." Her mother said, "Gigi, I realize that it was the devil that got into you, so I am going to have to switch him out of you,"—which she proceeded to do. About two hours later, Bea once again met her mother at the door. "Mrs. Graham, I don't know what happened, but when you left, they went

and did the same thing again." Well, this time her mother went up the stairs two at a time with a little larger switch in hand. Gigi heard her coming and before her mother even reached the top stair she started in. "Mother, Mother, you can't blame us, it was the devil again." Then she saw her mother's face and the switch and quickly added, "But, Mother, as soon as he saw you coming, he left." So, you see what we mean when we say that everyone should have a Gigi. Today we look at her in amazement. An instinctive homemaker, all she has ever wanted to do was to marry, raise a family, and serve the Lord all at the same time—which is exactly what she has been doing ever since she married Stephan Tchividjian at the age of seventeen. They have lived in at least twelve different homes in four countries, from Switzerland to Israel, from a trailer to a home in Florida; loving one another, loving their children and grandchildren, and loving home—for home is an atmosphere rather than a place. If ever a person was qualified to pass on what she has learned along the way, Gigi is. She has taught us both so much—for which we will be eternally grateful.

Billy and Ruth Graham

Mother, Daddy and me.
Me as a young child (left)

Therefore everyone who has heard these words of mine and puts them into practice is like a wise man who built his house on the rock. The rain came down, the streams rose, and the winds blew and beat against that house. Yet it did not fall because it had its foundation on the rock.

(Matthew 7: 24-25)

Passing It On

The sound of crunching gravel beneath the tires suddenly brought me back to reality. I had been remembering…remembering my happy childhood, as we made our way up the driveway leading to the familiar, red brick farmhouse. With a heavy heart I slowly got out of the car. I always disliked good-byes, but this one was going to be even more difficult than usual. I knew that this would be the last time I would see my grandmother Graham.

One by one we approached her bedside. Taking each one in her feeble arms, she gave us a special verse or a blessing and then with deep conviction in her weak voice she said, "Pass it on." A few days later "Mother Graham" died. But I have never forgotten her words.

As we entered her quiet, cool bedroom, tears filled my eyes. She looked so small and frail sitting on the edge of her bed. Soft white hair framed her sweet, gentle face, which, although pale, was radiant with the joy of seeing her grandchildren and great-grandchildren again.

The book that you now hold in your hands is part of the spiritual heritage God gave me. The pages mark passages in our own family's faith journey through the years. We have had our ups and downs, our difficulties, our problems, but God has been faithful. May God encourage you through these words and pictures to continue—or perhaps begin—a spiritual inheritance that will outlive you, bringing strength and joy to your children's children.

Mother Graham encouraging great-granddaughter Jerushah to "Pass it on."
Mother and Daddy Graham (left)

My wedding on May 3, 1963

1

Choosing Wisely

You did not choose me but I chose you and appointed you to go and bear fruit— fruit that will last.

(John 15:16)

Getting married and having a large family was what I desired. At an early age, with much counsel from my family and with my parents' full approval, I made the decision to marry by focusing on the faithfulness of God. Stephan and I entered marriage with a firm conviction that we were making a lifelong commitment. That doesn't mean it's been easy. Far from it! But our marriage began on a firm foundation of mutual faith in God.

Ever since I was a small girl, Mother and Daddy suggested I pray for my future life's partner. The boy I was going to marry someday, they explained, was approximately my age and— somewhere in the world—was going through the same kinds of problems and struggles as I. Because I followed my parents' teaching and prayed for my future husband, it never occurred to me that I might miss the right one when he came along. I also told the Lord I would not marry anyone until my immediate family agreed. I was claiming a verse I had memorized years before. "He makes those of the same house one accord." Because I had a godly family and valued my heritage, I firmly believed what Stephan told me in his proposal letter. He wrote that "the same Spirit says the same thing." That sentence, in fact, is inscribed in our wedding bands.

Mother and Daddy's engagement photo

If this marriage was part of His plan, then His Holy Spirit would give assurance to all of my family. Beginning married life on a solid foundation doesn't mean you will somehow dodge all the ups and downs, struggles and adjustments.

Stephan is from an Armenian-European background, and I from a small American town in the rural South. When we were first married, it was like a high-hurdles race, one cultural obstacle after another.

We were married in Switzerland and made our home there. I didn't speak a word of French and, with family and friends thousands of miles away, it wasn't long before I became homesick. Tensions would build up, background differences had to be worked out, and a few heated arguments began to boil to the surface. The honeymoon high was soon exchanged for the realities of married life. As the words to one Southern song so aptly put it, "It is so easy to get married but hard to be wed."

We lived in a house on the side of a mountain overlooking the Swiss Alps. It was a very romantic setting, especially when the full moon would slide up from behind the mountains and shine down on our little valley. But even this lovely fairy tale setting with all its beauty could not make two very different individuals from such completely different backgrounds adjust without a little difficulty here and there.

My son Stephan Nelson & Lisa with Daddy

My daughter Berdjette & David Barker

My son Basyle & Lydia with Stephan & me

My wedding day

19

I am one of those people who takes Ephesians 4:26 at face value; I don't like the sun to go down while I am still angry. I like to settle things before I go to sleep at night—even if it means waking my husband up at night to finish a fight! When we first married, Stephan would walk out the door to get away and cool off after—or worse yet, *during*—an argument.

This would infuriate me because he would leave me alone with my anger—and the kids. At the time, we had only one car. And he would go after those car keys.

When it became apparent early in Daddy's

ministry that he was going to be away from

home much of the time, he decided to let

Mother choose where she would like to live.

She chose a little cove in the mountains of

North Carolina called Montreat.

I vividly remember one such argument in our bedroom one night overlooking those serene, moonlit Alps. I looked in his eyes and saw right away that he was going after the keys. This time I got to them first.

We lived on the side of a mountain and had a balcony. I went to the window, stepped onto that balcony, and threw those keys as hard and far as I could. We never did find them.

The choices moms and dads make today about home and family have solemn, life-shaping implications. My mother made a wise but difficult choice to live near her family and not travel all over the world with Daddy. For Daddy's part, even with all the Lord has accomplished through him over the years, I think he would say he wishes he had spent more time with his children, and made that a priority in his life. He now encourages young parents to do just that.

When it became apparent early in Daddy's ministry that he was going to be away from home much of the time, he decided to let Mother choose where she would like to live. She chose a little cove in the mountains of North Carolina called Montreat.

It was a small community, comprised largely of retired Presbyterian missionaries and pastors in the winter months and a conference center in the summer months.

She chose this little place because my grandfather, a retired medical missionary and surgeon, still had a practice in Asheville not too far away, and he and Lao Niang, my maternal grandparents, had chosen Montreat as their home. With Daddy away so often, Mother felt it would be wise to settle near her parents. So they bought and lived in the little house right across the street from my grandparents, where I now have the joy of spending several weeks a year with my children.

The years have proven over and over again that the Holy Spirit was guiding Mother in that important decision. I grew up knowing all the privileges and blessings of the extended family. Any time I wished, I could run to my grandparents, over the little stream, across the lane, and down to their back

A happy family reunion

Mother trying to teach me to cook

door…which was never locked.

My grandparents made it an integral part of their ministry to help Mother raise the children. I struggle to express how grateful I am for the influence my grandparents had on my values and character. My Christian heritage was further enriched by the contacts I had with all the dear saints of God who lived in our small community. Daddy's parents weren't far away, either—just two hours away on a little dairy farm.

I hear many confess that life is so hectic they rarely even eat together as a family. Each one is off in a thousand and one activities and directions.

How then are we to know one another? Do we really have any idea what makes the other members of our family happy? Or if someone is struggling through some deep hurt? Or what their goals and values are—and how those goals and values might have changed within the last few weeks or months?

Edith Schaeffer compares a family to a mobile: constantly moving, constantly changing, yet within the framework of a form. She says a family is "unity and diversity, form and freedom, togetherness and individuality, and a Christian family is a mobile blown by the gentle breeze of the Holy Spirit."

Families today most certainly are moving and changing. But we are losing the framework and the form. Traditions no longer have the same influence or magnetic tug. Values are changing. Absolutes are hard to find. Roles and responsibilities are confused and bewildering. Heritage is a word from some distant, irrelevant past. Authority and respect are fading from our vocabularies.

Modern conveniences may spare us from much of the traditional work in a home, but today's culture has added incredible burdens and pressures on the family. The pressure for father to succeed and get ahead. The pressure for mother to bring home a second income and find fulfillment outside the home. The pressure for the kids to do well in school, resist negative peer pressure in a drug- and sex-saturated culture, and carve out some kind of self-concept amidst all the confusion. And all of this on top of the everyday tensions and frictions of a normal home life!

I hear many confess that life is so hectic they rarely even eat together as a family. Each one is off in a thousand and one activities and directions.

So many of these burdens are totally foreign to the home atmosphere in which I grew up years ago. Yet as a mother of seven and grandmother of four living in a large American city, I now face many of these tensions. The more problems I face, the more grateful I become for the home life and heritage I was privileged to receive back in the mountains of North Carolina.

We all face a lifetime of choices. The Bible speaks of the broad road that leads to destruction and the narrow path that leads to life. In old depictions of this word picture, we see that narrow path winding off through the thornbushes into the distant hills. In reality, it is more like a little bicycle path going down the middle of a ten-lane freeway—in the

Mother always taught me, with a twinkle in her eye, "There are times to quit submitting and start outwitting."

opposite direction. So when we talk about the path of life that pleases God, so often it is contrary to everything around us. We must cling to our commitments and maintain our balance in the middle of a culture that is screaming by in the opposite direction! Yet, when we look up the path ahead of us, we see that we are not alone. Christ is our great example. He is the One we are following.

A homemaker recently said to me wistfully, "I wish that I had a ministry."

Ministry is just a fancy word for servanthood. In that context, I find I have a multitude of opportunities to minister. Now, I admit that I don't always take them, but they are there right under my nose. If I am honest with myself, I will usually have to acknowledge that the reason I don't see them is I am so frequently preoccupied with self. Realizing this, I must come back to the Lord again and again to seek His forgiveness. Wrapping myself afresh in His selfless love, I take another look around and discover unlimited opportunities to serve.

In the home, we have three basic ministries.

First, we have a ministry to our mate.

There are no pat formulas for a happy marriage. That would be nice, but it just isn't that easy. There are many wonderful principles and many good practical suggestions, but no simple A-B-C procedures. Each couple's needs are different. Each family situation is unique. But everyone has the need to be loved, to be appreciated, needed, and encouraged.

Before I married, I was told by a dear Christian woman with six children that I could ask for nothing more than a Christian gentleman for a husband. And that is exactly what the Lord gave me. If you have this kind of a man, don't take him for granted.

Perhaps you have a difficult marriage. Your husband may be an alcoholic, a wanderer, or just plain unappreciative. Mother often told us that she thought it was our job as wives to make our husbands happy, and that it was God's job to make them good. The story is told about the wife of Disraeli, one of Queen Victoria's prime ministers, who was a much older woman, very wealthy, and quite unattractive. In writing a book about her husband, she said, "Dizzy married me for money, but if he had it to do over again, he would marry me for love." She didn't try to make him good, only as happy as she could, and she was rewarded. Would your mate choose to marry you again?

Many problems in marriage stem from the fact that we expect our mates to be only what Jesus Christ can be to us. Only Christ can totally satisfy us, fulfill our needs, and be everything to us. In fact, no other person or thing on earth can be to you what God wants His Son Jesus Christ to be to you.

We're only human, and we've all been affected by the Fall of Man. I so often forget this, and expect Stephan to do for me what I should be allowing Christ to do. Part of being a suitable helper is realizing that our husbands have needs, too, and looking for ways to satisfy and fulfill those needs instead of expecting them to constantly fulfill ours.

For women married to difficult men, life can seem lonely at times; sometimes it will seem that you are forever on the giving end of the relationship. The alternatives, however, are also grim…and the rewards of allowing Jesus Christ to be your all in all cannot be measured.

He can be your peace when there is no peace.

He can be your strength when you have no strength.

He can be your courage when you don't know how you will go on another day.

He can be your comfort when you feel abandoned or insecure.

Those who choose to rely and depend completely on Him will never be disappointed.

The second ministry I have as a homemaker is to our children.

Psalm 1:3 reads, "And he (or she) is like a tree planted by streams of water, which yields its fruit in season and whose leaf does not wither." One day the Lord spoke quite clearly in my heart and confirmed to me that my fruit-bearing season for now was at home with the children.

Daddy playing with grandchildren

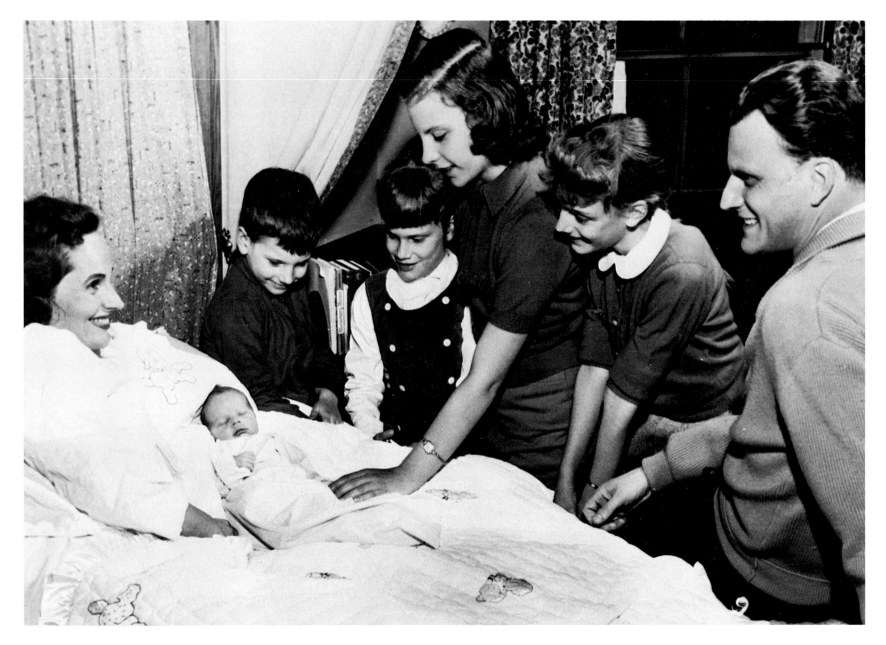

My sisters and brother and I meet our brother Ned

After a Sunday service, one of America's well-known pastors was approached by a mother with a string of little children behind her. She told this pastor she felt God was calling her to minister. He turned and gently pointed to her children. "Yes," he said, "and there is your congregation."

I was also taught the importance of ministering to the children by my mother. During our formative years, she took care of us almost exclusively. She didn't even teach a Bible study. As we left home and went out to begin lives and families of our own, she slowly began to add to and broaden this ministry. But, even now, if one of us or her grandchildren needs her, she does her best to come and meet that need.

It is never too early, nor is it ever too late, to begin ministering to your children. Jochabed and Hannah are two women in the Bible who have often been an encouragement to me. Jochabed was the mother of Moses, and Hannah the mother of Samuel. Both of these godly women had their little boys only until they were weaned, which in those days meant perhaps four or five years. Then Moses was sent to the immoral and affluent Egyptian court, and Samuel was sent to the temple to be trained and raised by an elderly priest who had not been able to train his own sons. Yet both Moses and Samuel grew to become powerful men of God.

Perhaps for different reasons, you have not been able to begin this early training of your children in the Lord. Perhaps you didn't know the Lord. For whatever reason you may have, this little illustration may encourage and help you. Years ago in England, a group of friends met in a pub after a hunt. They were talking and laughing and recounting the day's activities. One hunter, excited, began to recount his story using sweeping gestures. Suddenly he hit a cup of tea and sent it splashing over the beautifully whitewashed wall.

He was terribly embarrassed, but before he could even apologize, one of the other men jumped to his feet, pulled a pen from his pocket, and began to sketch on the wall. As he sketched, a magnificent, majestic stag began to emerge from what was just a stain on the wall.

That man was Landseer, England's foremost painter of wildlife. If Landseer could do that with an ugly tea stain, how much more can the Creator God make something beautiful out of all our faults and failures if we will just yield our lives to Him. God loves to make a miracle out of a mess! A pastor friend of ours recently said, "A problem is a platform from which God can do a miracle."

Mother's constant reference point in a sometimes chaotic household was her love for and dependence upon Scripture.

My father, away from home so much of the time, left most of the responsibilities and burdens of rearing five children to my mother. In an interview, she was once asked how she had done it. She replied very simply, "On my knees." Andrew Murray calls that our "dependent posture." Although Daddy was not home every evening, when he was home, he led us in daily Bible reading and prayer. How precious it was to have him take his role as spiritual leader seriously! He practiced at home what he preached in public. Children need to see fathers on their knees, acknowledging and bowing to a higher authority and loving their mother.

Mother's constant reference point in a sometimes chaotic household was her love for and dependence upon Scripture. She may not have had the luxury of long quiet times or elaborate Bible studies, but you could usually find her Bible propped open in a prominent place as she worked, on the ironing board, by the sink, on the kitchen counter. She would glean a verse or two and meditate on it all day.

Memories of girlhood—my sisters and I share happy times

We can all do that; we can raise our children in a dependent posture—on our knees—leaning on God's Word for wisdom and encouragement. What a privilege to have been raised by a mother and father who spent so much of their time on their knees for us! Now I falteringly try to follow their example.

The third ministry I have as a homemaker is to my community.

The best way to accomplish that is to be an example by tending our own gardens well, by being a "sweet-smelling savor." Does your garden invite inquiries as to why and how it is so pleasing?

My mother tells a story about me that illustrates this point. When we were all small, one morning before school, she realized she had overslept. She jumped out of bed and threw on her robe and slippers. Without even taking time to comb her hair, she grabbed my little brother from his crib—dirty diaper and all—and rushed into the kitchen to prepare our breakfast. My sister Bunny bounced downstairs in a jovial mood, chattering nonstop. In contrast to Bunny, I've always been slow to get going in the morning and need to get my blood circulating before I even become civil.

I arrived on this scene and sat down to eat my breakfast. After a few minutes, I'd had enough. I threw down my fork, pushed my chair back, stood up, and said, "Mother, between looking at you, smelling Franklin, and listening to Bunny, I am just not hungry."

Many younger couples are looking at us older Christians and established families and are not finding themselves hungry for what we have. Several years ago my oldest daughter watched me coming unglued as I struggled to get the younger ones to bed. "Mama," she said, "you've yet to convince me that children can be a blessing." But she must have seen something to like—she's now building a family of her own!

A family walk in Switzerland, 1960

Me holding baby brother Ned

Family photo with two of our pets in the early 1960s and, as so often the case, Daddy was away from home

With seven children in the household in times past, there was quite a bit of noise—and not all of it sweet and pleasant. I have often thought about putting a sign out in our yard like the one seen in a hotel lobby:

SORRY FOR THE NOISE AND INCONVENIENCE, BUT WE ARE GROWING!

Our task is not to showcase perfect families within our communities. Our task is to allow an unbelieving world to see a real family struggling with real issues yet finding strength and wisdom in a loving, sufficient, Savior.

I recently heard a psychologist say that one of the main reasons families, especially Christian families, were dysfunctional was that they were more interested in maintaining an image than in solving a problem. We are tempted for one reason or another to try to hide the faults and failures in our family. But, let us not make the terrible mistake of being so concerned about our image, our standing in the community, our reputation, etc., that we don't work on or seek help in solving our problems.

These ministries to my husband, my children, and my community are the three basic ministries in my life now. But we don't always see immediate results to our labors.

The work we do today needs doing again tomorrow.

The floor we clean today is trampled and dirty a few hours later.

The clothes we washed yesterday are in a pile on the floor and need washing again.

The dinner we slave over for several hours is devoured in minutes.

The bills we pay this month need paying again next month.

The correction and instruction we gave yesterday needs restating and reminding today.

As parents, we don't receive promotions or raises. We don't get annual reviews to help us evaluate our performance. Many years of reminding, disciplining, schooling, loving, and encouraging pass before we begin to see the fruits of our labors.

But if we take the time to notice, there are daily wages. The little dirty kiss planted on our cheek for no apparent reason. The unexpected thank you from our teenager. The sheer pleasure of seeing the image of God bud and blossom in a growing child. The awesome moment when we hear our child's first solo attempt to talk to the heavenly Father.

Some kinds of wages will never appear on a tax form.

Some kinds of wages last forever.

St. Matthew says that Jesus did not come to be served, but to serve. If I am trying to serve in God's way, unselfishly, I find that I have little time to think of myself. I learned this, too, from the example of my family.

I don't think it ever occurred to either my parents or grandparents to think of themselves first—or even to think of themselves much at all.

A psychologist friend of ours says that the word "trapped" describes the feelings of so many of his patients. He then defines "trapped" as a preoccupation with the personal pronouns: Me, Myself; My life, My choices, My opportunities, My time, My need for this, My desire for that.

Most of us are too preoccupied with ourselves.

Over the last twenty years, we have been inundated with words like freedom, "identity," "fulfillment," and "self-assertion." None of these concepts are bad in themselves. But when I find these words creeping into my thoughts ahead of the Lord Jesus Christ, or into the responsibilities and ministries He has given me to do, then I take caution. I try to find a little time to take an internal inventory of my priorities, goals, and the real desires of my heart (watching out for the devil's old trick of "morbid introspection"). Most of all, I must determine if these things are glorifying God and if they are fitting into His plan for my life.

I married at seventeen and never finished college. When we came back to the States and my husband resumed studies toward his doctorate, I felt some pressure to go back to college and pick up a few courses.

I had three children at the time, and was pregnant with my fourth. I had no help at home. My husband was a busy father and student. I was determined to make "A's," which I did, but I had to study hard, clean house, cook, and put up with morning sickness as well as continue to be a good wife and mother.

One day I asked myself what my motives were. I'd started out with good reasons. I love to learn and study. I wanted to increase my knowledge and not let my husband outgrow me. But as time went on, pride crept in. People kept patting me on the back and saying, "How do you do it all? How do you make "A's," take care of a home and children—and even continue to look nice?"

I began to relish this attention. Before long, it began to interfere with my priorities—something had to change. I thought back to the original priority of my family, examined my motives and adjusted my day's schedule. I didn't drop all of my classes, but I did cut down and make adjustments.

Dr. Larry Crabb has said, "The real block to self-fulfillment is a preoccupation with self."

David said to the Lord, "My contentment is…in…knowing all is well between us" (Psalm 17: 15, TLB).

We find fulfillment when we are filled with the Holy Spirit.

We find fulfillment when we are doing what we were created to do.

The Westminster catechism states that "man's

Daddy's 70th birthday celebration

chief end is to glorify God and to enjoy Him forever."

That is fulfillment.

I am often asked, "Isn't it hard to be the daughter of a famous man?" or, "What is it like to be the daughter of such a famous person?" To be honest, I've never been much bothered by those thoughts. It was instilled in me from the earliest memory that I was to seek my identity in God and His will for my life. Anything else would be identity spelled with a capital I.

Basyle & Lydia with Stephan & me upon their graduation from University 1990

As Paul says in Galatians, "I no longer live, but Christ lives in me." Matthew 10: 39 teaches that the more we lose our lives, the more we will find them. This has been true in my life. In the times when I was preoccupied with myself, I found days slipping by with little sense of significance or fulfillment. Time was passing through my fingers, and I was losing or wasting it.

But each time He reminded me, gently but firmly, that this was not His will nor way for me. Graciously nudging me back to reality, He would draw me back into a wholehearted preoccupation with Him and the ministries He had placed in my hands. Once again, I would begin to sense what real living was all about. Not just existing from day to day, but living each day to the fullest. For Him.

I used to read Proverbs 31 and begin to feel intimidated—even guilty. This woman was gifted, industrious, virtuous, organized, strong—the original bionic woman.

But then I began taking a closer look. It finally dawned on me that her accomplishments were achieved over a lifetime, not in a week, or a month, or even a few short years. She was a faithful woman whose careful choices and creative use of God's time and gifts reaped a lifetime of rich rewards.

Proverbs 31 closes with these accolades: "Her children arise and call her blessed; her husband also, as he praises her: 'Many women do noble things, but you surpass them all.'"

What a great reward! What wonderful words! But I can think of still better ones. They are the words I long to hear as I step out of this brief life and meet my Lord at the gate of eternity.

"Well done, good and faithful servant!"

Mother and Daddy with grandchildren acting "normal"

Me playing with my first grandchild, Stetson

2

Taking Time

There is a time for everything.

A time to weep...a time to laugh...

A time to embrace...a time to love...

A time to be silent....a time to speak...

A time to keep...a time to throw away...

(Ecclesiastes 3: 1-8)

Deuteronomy 6 directs parents to pass along their spiritual heritage throughout the course of any given day: "When you sit at home and when you walk along the road, when you lie down and when you get up."

Today that translates to "when you're working in the kitchen, carpooling to school, sitting around the breakfast table, or watching TV in the evenings."

The craziest subjects come up in our home at the least likely times: like a critical point of sex education in the midst of cleaning the kitchen. Or like a question about professional athletes who have the AIDS virus, or the consequences of violating God's standards while in the left-turn lane of a busy intersection on the way to a school program. Or like a penetrating spiritual insight while we're frantically packing the car for a trip to North Carolina.

There really are no set times or specific locations to pass on our values and spiritual legacy. If it's left to Sunday mornings or an after-supper structured devotional, the handoff may never happen at all.

Daddy leading my sisters and me in family prayer at home

The Deuteronomy passage implies a life-style of modeling and discussing those things that are most deeply important to us. If it isn't something that's woven through the everyday cloth of normal living, then it is weak fabric indeed. We cannot hope that it will stand up to the strains and stresses of today's cultural pressures. The times we live in work against the priority of passing along a spiritual heritage. Yet there has never been a more critical hour in which to do that! In a kinder, gentler time, the winds of our culture weren't blowing so hard, so cruelly. Families today need roots more than ever to keep from being blown away! Yet we are spending less and less time with one another. We must learn to maximize our moments together.

Let's face it, most of us aren't going to be able to change our lives radically. We can't transform the times we live in. We can't go back to the good old days. We can't all grow up in a small Chinese mission compound as my Mother did. We can't spend our childhood days in a sleepy mountain hamlet in North Carolina as I did. We can't all draw on tranquil summer memories of a mountainside chalet in the Alps as my two oldest children can.

Gary Trudeau says he is looking for a life-style that doesn't require his presence. This may sound wonderful, but it really isn't feasible, is it? We've got to think how we are going to incorporate the Bible's priceless spiritual principles into the busy, hectic lives we live.

It's a little here, a little there. If you go out for breakfast with one of your children, don't bury your

At home in Florida with my children Jerushah, Tullian and Antony

face in the newspaper while you wait for your pancakes. If you have to drive across town with one of your kids to pick something up, don't drown out conversation with the radio. If you take the time to watch a TV program together, don't immediately get up and head for the fridge as soon as it's over. Maximize the time by talking about the program, perhaps giving a biblical perspective.

Families must face this unyielding reality: making a priority of spending time together will not happen without sacrifice.

When my oldest son was in high school, for example, he gave up a position on the tennis team because it would have meant missing supper every night with the family. That's not something Stephan and I could have imposed on him—even if we'd wanted to. It was his decision. He had to weigh the alternatives. He had to make the sacrifice.

When I was very young, my Mother and Daddy made all our decisions for us with our best interests in mind. Then, as we grew older, we learned to make these decisions together.

We all work at whatever we value. Some of my friends work hard at the office. Others at golf. It depends on what you count most important. My husband and I value our relationship with each other. Stephan is my best friend, but we've still had to work at finding time to be together. It's meant personal sacrifice. It's meant giving up certain activities or diversions we might have enjoyed. It's meant surrendering opportunities for extra income or material things that would have been wonderful to possess.

But what we've given up doesn't compare to what we've gained over the years.

Because of this time together, my mind has been enlarged greatly. My husband has taught me so much and has brought so much into my life from his background and wide experience. When we disagree, we spend time talking it over, and we try never to make a major decision until we are in agreement.

The greatest gift my husband has given to me, after his love and his total commitment, has been his gift of time. How can I ever forget the time when he walked into the kitchen for breakfast and saw me standing at the sink, in tears. He walked over to the telephone, called his secretary, and said, "Cancel all · my appointments today, I'm staying home."

"But, Stephan," I said, "all your clients...."

"Today you need me more than my clients do," he said, wrapping his arms around me.

Every couple should find time to take vacations together. Now for some, this might mean expensive vacation trips each year. For most of us, however, it probably means a night or a weekend at a nearby hotel—or maybe just staying at home and sending the kids to some friends for a night. You would be astonished how quiet the house can be! On one

Me with Stephan Nelson
August 1965

Me as a young child

Antony helping decorate the
Christmas tree

Jerushah shares a moment with
Mother & Daddy before a crusade

41

Daddy talking to grandbaby Antony

such night, I noticed the ticking of the grandfather clock and the hum of the refrigerator. I don't think I had ever heard those sounds before.

The important thing is to be together and to be alone.
Alone to love.
Alone to talk.
Alone to reminisce.
Alone to dream.
Alone to pray.
Alone to sketch future plans and goals.

There are many practical ways of spending time together as family members without making elaborate plans. A daughter can help her mom with the dishes. A father can take a child along when he runs Saturday errands. A whole family can work together in the yard.

When we lived up north, raking leaves wasn't one of our favorite jobs, but we made it a fun family time. Making large piles, then jumping from a tree into the pile is fun. Putting a few twigs in with the leaves makes a cozy fire for roasting hot dogs and marshmallows and for taking the chill off as the fall air gets cooler toward late afternoon.

I can't think of a place I would rather have been when I was growing up than home. I am so thrilled that my husband and our children feel the same way.

Most of us wake up in a hurry—then gain momentum as the day progresses! I've wondered if part of our constant activity is simply self-protection against convicting thoughts—thinking through our sacred responsibilities before God. Dr. Howard Hendricks hits closer to the truth than most of us would like to admit when he calls our incessant busyness "a cheap narcotic to deaden the pain of an empty life."

I've been suspicious for a number of years that the whole universe is speeding up. The days seem shorter. So do the nights. So do the weekends. So do my publisher's deadlines. Time to accomplish most anything seems in ever shorter supply.

It has been well said that if the devil can't make you bad, then he will make you busy. He knows how to best trip us up, doesn't he? It might not occur to me to have an affair. It might not occur to me to abuse one of my children physically. It might not occur to me to go to the local department store and steal my favorite dress off the rack. But I do get too busy. And when I get busy, I tend to lose my temper more easily and to struggle with the resulting tension.

I've been suspicious for a number of years that the whole universe is speeding up. The days seem shorter. So do the nights. So do the weekends.

A friend of ours used to say, "Any activity that is not led of the Holy Spirit is just a bunch of busyness." So much of what we find ourselves involved with in a given week is just that—a bunch of busyness. In the biblical story of Mary and Martha, Martha wasn't rebuked by the Lord for setting the table. Or cooking. Or sweeping the floor. Or decorating the house. She wasn't doing anything wrong. Things do have to get done! It was just that her priorities were in the wrong place at the wrong time.

Busy with good things, she missed her opportunity for the best thing.

When I asked my thirteen-year-old what a home was, he answered, "A home is a place where we find direction." I found this true in my childhood home.

When I was very young, my Mother and Daddy made all our decisions for us with our best interests in mind. Then, as we grew older, we learned to make these decisions together. My husband says he felt it was important to teach our children to listen to their consciences. If we, as parents, continued to make all their decisions for them, he said, their own consciences would become weak and lazy.

Daddy saying one of his many good-byes

My parents were very strong on such moral issues as honesty, purity, and respect for elders. But minor things that came up as we were growing up— for example, the length of hair or taste in clothing— were never made issues. They stuck to all the important, bedrock, biblical concerns.

They respected our individuality and our privacy. My parents never entered my bedroom without knocking. They never read my letters, notes from boyfriends, or my diary. They never listened in on my conversations on the telephone. They treated us with respect.

There were five of us, each very different. One of my brothers went through a time when he loved rock music—at least to Mother it was rock. So she made a deal with him.

"All right, Franklin," she said, "I'll tell you what. You can listen to your rock music, but in your bedroom with the door closed. Please don't have it blaring all over the house."

Thinking that issue settled, Mother left the house. A short while later she returned with thirty missionary ladies for tea. She opened the front door and was greeted with a blast of Franklin's rock music. Furious, she went flying up the stairs, two at a time. My brother wasn't even in his room. He had just left his door open, the record on, blaring away. As punishment, Mother confiscated all his records.

That night, however, her conscience began to bother her. The next day she got into the car, drove to Asheville, found a record store, and bought an album by Franklin's favorite group. She gave it to him that night, then sat down on his bed, and listened to it with him. Then they discussed it. That's communication.

We were always free to talk to our parents about anything, and we were always permitted to disagree respectfully. If they believed they had been wrong, they admitted it.

I have a saying on a plaque above my desk. It's an attitude I learned at home:

Lord, when we are wrong, make us willing to change; and when we are right, make us easy to live with.

Nothing replaces time together as a family.

There is no way we can have real communication in our families today in this complex society in which we live, if we do not take time. Some say that it is quality and not quantity of time that matters. In today's world, I'm not sure I agree with that.

I don't believe anything replaces time together.

Time to talk.
Time to play.
Time to disagree.
Time to share, to love, to get to know one another.
Time to understand one another's hurts and hopes and dreams and fears.
Time just to be there for each other.
Time to catch the first little signs or clues that something is wrong so that you can work together before it becomes a major problem.

Most likely we will never find this time. We will simply have to make it.

My mother was always home. I used to take that for granted. No longer.

She sacrificed traveling, speaking, teaching, and—most of all—being with Daddy, to be there with us, to be available. There were times when she must have wondered if it was worth it. I have asked myself, Why do you make those homemade cookies from scratch when the kids would be just as happy with store-bought? Or, Why do you continue to clean little boys' rooms and bathrooms when they seem to be just as content living in a mess?

The results of self-sacrifice for a mother may not be seen for many years. So much toil seems to go unnoticed or unappreciated. Nevertheless, the rewards are there…or will be.

It is worth it all when your ten-year-old tells you that he likes having you at home when he returns from school, and that he wouldn't look forward to coming home if you were not there—that he likes running in to tell of all the day's activities, all the little, seemingly unimportant incidents.

As I look back, I have many regrets that I didn't do more little things with my children. My kids would say things like, "Mom, please help me put this puzzle together," and that was the last thing I wanted to do. I have regrets that I didn't spend more time reading with them. Or just playing with them. Or listening to their jokes. Or taking time to

Berdjette & her husband with their son sharing a special time together

Me with grandchild Stetson

Two of my grandchildren, Seth and Charlee, play hide-and-go-seek

Granddaughter Charlee asleep on Papa T's shoulder

Me with Stephan, my sweetheart and my best friend

look at something that was important to them.

It's the little things that count.

Life is made up of little things, isn't it? I don't think it's the big things that lodge in our memories the way the little things do.

I remember being in the middle of laundry one afternoon, and just staggering through the sheer drudgery of getting it done when my three-year-old came in and yelled, "Mom! You've got to come quickly! I want to show you something."

I didn't want to leave my job half finished, and I tried to put him off with a just-a-minute-honey. But finally I gave in. He grabbed my hand with his little hand and rushed me down to the lakeside to see some baby ducks.

Well, many big things have come and gone since that incident years ago. Funny how that moment lingers in my mind. Funny how that scene stays etched in my memory. I wouldn't trade it for anything you could offer me. My precious little three-year-old…golden blond curls shining in the sunshine, ruffled by the wind…the excited piping of his little voice…the closeness of that moment, holding hands, beholding something of God's handiwork. Together.

And I came so close to missing it.

Time together does take conscious effort. This is a priority. And one that needs renewing a dozen times a day. The big things come and go; they wash through our earthly pilgrimage like massive waves, and our lives rise and fall and somehow continue to bob along through each one. But from eternity's point of view, when the value of our lives is finally tallied before His throne, I have a feeling it's the little things that will count the most.

My parents always had time for me when I was small. I don't ever remember going to my father's office and being told that he was too busy. He made me feel secure. Significant. Loved.

So many times it's the interruptions that irritate us. Yet as you review the life of Christ in the gospels, it seems like half His ministry sprang out of interruptions. He was on His way to one place or another when someone would stop Him. Ask Him a question. Challenge Him. Threaten Him. Bless Him. Cry out to Him. Try to touch Him. Beg Him to go in a different direction.

I wonder how He views the interruptions in our lives. Could it be that taking time for the little child nagging you with a question is more important from eternity's perspective than working on a magazine article or playing a tennis match or attending a PTA committee meeting?

So much of a compelling home life is an attitude and an atmosphere. The people I grew up around were mostly pastors or missionaries. None of them had money. What they possessed did not have a high worldly value. What they passed on to me was not material. It was an attitude.

Daddy takes time to enjoy his grandchild

The problem comes when interruptions interrupt our interruptions! And that's the way our household is so much of the time.

But as I've considered these interruptions, I've finally begun to realize that you can't really plan memorable moments with your children. You can't program those spontaneous conversations. You can't manufacture those moments of closeness. They simply come in the middle of doing something else! What we need from the Lord is the grace and humility to admit that something could be more important than our agenda for the day.

It doesn't mean we don't plan. Plans are important. But we must be submissive to the Lord in the midst of those plans, realizing that He might have something better! My mother always said, "Hang loose and play it by ear." By those standards, she was a very loose woman!

So much of a compelling home life is an attitude and an atmosphere. The people I grew up around were mostly retired pastors or missionaries. None of them had money. What they possessed did not have a high worldly value. What they passed on to me was not material. It was an attitude. A way of looking at life. A wealth of Christian experience. They not only knew how to minister, they knew how to play hard and how to relax. They were happy, fun-loving Christians and whetted my appetite for what they had.

There should be fun and humor and, yes, even the ability to laugh at ourselves.

My maternal grandmother, Lao Niang, suffered from migraine headaches all her life, so there were times when she tended to be a little short-tempered or snippy. My grandfather would diffuse those moments with humor. There could have been a lot of tension in the home if he hadn't had a sense of humor. We always know when Daddy is getting too tired; he begins to lose his ability to laugh.

I once asked my Mother, "What kinds of things did the missionaries in China do for fun?"

There they were, in the depths of China in a little village surrounded by bandits and warlords. And what did they do? They built a swimming pool on the compound. And a tennis court! (Very simple ones, of course.)

Somehow they felt swimming and tennis to be important in the midst of bringing salvation into China.

Cousins having fun rafting

Mother tells the story of the Chinese watching the missionaries sweating and straining and puffing as they played set after set of tennis. The Chinese watched solemnly by the hour, their eyes going back and forth.

One Chinese man could stand it no longer. He approached one of the missionaries and said, "Excuse me, sir, but can't you hire somebody to hit that ball back and forth for you?"

Much of the love my Mother has for books stems from evenings in China when these missionaries would gather in one home. The women would teach how to do handiwork, and the men took turns reading the classics out loud.

One priceless heritage builder we can all afford is a simple photo album. With an inexpensive camera and a determination to capture some of the fun...

Life on that mission field during these years was never easy—but it certainly wasn't grim! These Christian ambassadors to China knew how to celebrate. Birthday parties. Holidays. Dress-up dinners. Mother remembers lots of laughter. And she still talks about the birthday party where two live ducks swam around in a table centerpiece then opened and closed their beaks in unison during the singing of "Happy Birthday."

I would say to those of you who can't look back on happy childhood memories that you should make some happy memories for your children—beginning now. It doesn't matter if they're your own kids, your grandkids, your nephews and nieces, or kids from your church or neighborhood. The past cannot be undone, but you can begin creating happy memories today. The more you do, the more the bad or bitter recollections will fade into the background.

I was talking recently about growing up in our family. I said, "Mother, I can think of very few mistakes you and Daddy made in raising us. The only thing I regret is that we were unable to do more things together as a family."

One trip we took as a family, to Switzerland, was so important to me as a fourteen-year-old. It has always stood out in my mind as a life-defining experience.

Kids tend to look back on certain camping trips or family activities and see them as bigger or more special than they really were—at least from parents' perspective. This includes even the trips where absolutely everything went wrong. To this day my adult children laugh about a few days that I would like to, somehow, permanently erase from my life's videotape. To me, they were unqualified disasters, but the kids make it sound like it was this wonderful family bonding time. Maybe they have a better perspective on those moments than I do!

The importance of doing things together simply cannot be measured. Yes, stick to your budget, but…sometimes you can't afford not to carve out time to make a memory. We've only gone white-water rafting once as a family, but we still talk about it!

Each year we make our pilgrimage back to Montreat, North Carolina. The kids all love being back at the little house where I grew up. It's fun to show them around my roots! The same little stream. The same trees where I played hide-and-seek. The

Relaxing at a local fair with my youngest son Antony and my eldest grandson Stetson

Daddy, my sister Anne and me with our favorite family pet Belshazzar, a Great Pyranees

Daddy with his first grandchild, Stephan Nelson

same spot where I parked my little brown tricycle. The same bridge I would race across to my grandparents' back door.

There is something warm and secure for all of us about relishing that continuity. Heritage really is something to hang on to.

One priceless heritage builder we can all afford is a simple photo album. With an inexpensive camera and a determination to capture some of the fun moments on film, you can create a book that will mean more to your family in future years than almost any other item in the house. I've heard a number of people say that the first thing they would save in a burning house (after all the people were out) would be their photo albums. Our albums have triggered endless laughs, groans, sighs, and trips down nostalgia lane. I believe they've given the children a personal sense of belonging and continuity. As they leaf through the pages, they feel their part and place in the flow of family history.

Proverbs 24: 3-4 says, "By wisdom a house is built, and through understanding it is established; through knowledge its rooms are filled with rare and beautiful treasures."

I have found that the kind of true wisdom that it takes to build a home can only come from God.

It is taking the time to know and understand my family and their needs that fills our home with "rare and beautiful treasures": riches like love, joy, happiness, understanding, acceptance, security, and direction.

All these precious and rare treasures, and more, I received in my little home in Montreat, North Carolina. And now, with the help of the Lord, I am passing this priceless legacy on to my children…and to theirs.

Daddy and grandson Stephan Nelson

3

Building a Heritage

For you have heard my vows. Oh God! You have given me the heritage of those who fear your name.

(Psalms 61: 5)

I become more convinced with every passing day that a dark, over-whelming storm has overtaken the family today. It is smashing into neighborhoods and homes across our country with unbelievable fury. Even those seeking God's will and God's best for their families are not exempt from its destructive power. In fact, we who refuse to bend to the fierce winds of this tempest will feel the greatest pressure. Someone has well said that the closer you get to Heaven, the more you will feel like Hell.

A few years ago massive earthquakes hit two major cities in Mexico. One struck Acapulco; the other, Mexico City. While Acapulco escaped with some minor damage—a few cracks here and there—huge sections of the capital city were flattened with terrible loss of life.

What made the difference? Acapulco was built on solid rock; Mexico City was constructed on the site of an ancient lake bed. When the shaking began, the hidden structures beneath those cities became apparent for all the world to see.

The Lord tells us to build our homes on a rock. To me, this means sinking our foundation posts deep into the bedrock of a spiritual heritage. Then, when the great storm breaks over the top of us, we won't be shaken loose or blown away.

Daddy with three of his great-grandchildren: Stetson, Charlee and Hope

But that doesn't mean there won't be a few cracks here and there after the dust settles!

It is frightening when you think about the lack of family role models today. My children look around them and just shake their heads. They have been disillusioned again and again when Christian couples and families they had admired and looked up to were shattered by unfaithfulness and divorce.

Where do we look for this Christian heritage we long to pass on to the next generation?

First, we need to look to the Lord Himself. He will never disappoint. He will never change like a shifting shadow. He will never make a sudden U-turn and leave us alone and abandoned at a crucial crossroads. He will never fail or forsake us. We need to go back to Him as a family. We need to cling to Him with all our strength. He is our Rock and our Fortress. He is our Strong Tower. In a sense, He is all the heritage we need.

But how wonderful if He has blessed you with a family legacy of godliness. It is an indescribable gift.

My home provided a storehouse of happy memories for me. The very form and framework of that home was my Christian heritage.

In Jeremiah we read, "Before I formed you in the womb, I knew you, before you were born I set you apart" (1:5). I believe that God knew me before I was shaped in the womb; that He had a plan for my life before I ever drew a breath. I do not believe for one moment that I was conceived by accident. Nor do I believe I was placed by accident into my family.

I was born into a family that prayed for me and loved me before I ever entered this world— especially since Mother and Daddy had been told

Standing left to right: Stetson, Charlee, Lisa, Stephan Nelson, Hope, David, Aram, Tullian, Lydia, Basyle.
Front: Seth, Berdjette, me, Antony.

My Mother, my friend

Stephan and me with Stephan Nelson,
Christmas 1964 in Switzerland

Stephan and me with Stetson

Mother and Daddy still in love
fifty years later

they would never be able to have children. All my aunts, uncles, and grandparents loved and served the Lord. They provided me with a vital, living example of what true Christianity is all about.

It is a life, a life of joyous commitment, not just a religion. I am continually awed by this wonderful legacy, though I realize it does not come without responsibility. The Bible says, in Luke 12: 48, "For everyone to whom much is given, from him much will be required." Again, in 1 Corinthians 4: 2, Paul writes, "Now it is required that those who have been given a trust must prove faithful."

In the Old Testament, we read of the godly heritage of Israel; and yet, we also read how frequently they failed and disappointed the Lord. I know that I fail Him often. I doubt or question at times. I struggle at other times. I have so far to go in my spiritual pilgrimage. But I will forever be grateful for my godly heritage.

As I was growing up, Sunday nights were very special family nights. My grandparents, who lived close to us and helped raise us, would come up every Sunday night for supper. Then we would gather around the piano and sing hymns and play Bible games. I learned a great deal about the Bible from those games.

There was always lots of humor and laughter. Tension was often broken by a joke. As a family, we always tried to see the humorous side of even very difficult situations. Although we were all verbal, strong-minded people given to arguments and lively discussions, we also accepted our differences of opinion and respected one another. We were taught by example that "a gentle answer turns away wrath, but a harsh word stirs up anger" (Proverbs 15:1).

Christianity was anything but a boring religion to me. It was an exciting way of life. When we had either personal or family problems, we were taught to talk them over with our heavenly Father. In fact, we were taught to talk to God about everything, from a major decision in our life, such as college or our future mates, to simply finding a parking space uptown.

In other words, our faith became a part of our everyday life. Even now I don't separate my spiritual life from my daily life. I talk to the Lord while I'm driving my car to the shopping center, while I'm washing dishes or vacuuming. I talk to the children about the Lord when I'm bathing them at night or when we're working in the garden together. Our love for Him cannot be separated from the ebb and flow of just plain living through the hours of the day.

When theologian Karl Barth was asked to name the most profound theological truth he knew, he replied, "Jesus loves me, this I know, for the Bible tells me so." This is theology that both Christians and sinners understand.

My heritage began before I was born, but it

There was always lots of humor and laughter. Tension was often broken by a joke, and we always, always tried to see the humorous side of even very difficult situations.

Me with sisters Anne and Bunny visiting Mother's birthplace in China, 1989

became a personal reality to me when, at the age of four, I gave my heart and life to Jesus Christ.

I was very ill, and my Mother worried that I might die. So she decided to tell me more about Jesus and how I could make Him a part of my life forever. She came to my room, sat beside me on the bed, and began to tell me how much God loved me. She explained that God loved me so very much that He sent His only Son Jesus Christ to die on the cross for me and to take away all of my badness. The only thing I had to do was to tell Him that I was sorry and ask Him to forgive my badness. If I would do that, He would come and live in my heart, and one day He would take me to Heaven to live with Him forever.

So I did just that. With a child's simple faith, I asked Jesus into my heart and life.

Looking back, I realize that I could have said no to Jesus that day; or later, as I became an adult, I could have dismissed that day as just another childish experience or something forced on me by my mother. But the Bible says that "he who began a good work in you will carry it on to completion until the day of Christ Jesus" (Philippians 1: 6). In other words, the Holy Spirit started something that day, and He will continue to prune and refine me until Jesus Himself returns, and "[I] shall be like Him for [I] shall see Him as He is" (1 John 3: 2).

So by the grace of God and the steadfast, faithful prayers of my godly family, I somehow think the devil didn't have a chance with me.

"Well, fine for you," people might say to me, "but I didn't happen to have Billy Graham for a dad. I didn't grow up in a Christian community. I didn't have missionary grandparents. I didn't inherit that kind of background—or anything close to it. What about me?"

I simply say again that God will be your heritage.

Scripture says that even if our father and mother should forsake us, the Lord will gladly receive us and teach us (see Psalm 27: 10-11).

All His saints from ages past are your heritage. Hebrews 12: 1 says that they watch you from the grandstands of Heaven and cheer you on.

Every believer has a rich heritage. If you don't find much to claim or encourage you in your immediate family background, it's time to look to your roots into the great family of believers across the world and down through history. It's time to celebrate your inheritance. It's time to find out where your true roots are. It's time to take delight in your heritage.

King David wrote: "As for the saints who are in the land, they are the glorious ones in whom is all my delight...surely I have a delightful inheritance" (Psalm 16: 3,6).

If you don't find much to claim or encourage you in your immediate family background, it's time to look to your roots into the great family of believers across the world and down through history.

According to the apostle Peter, we have a perfect inheritance waiting for us in Heaven—a treasure that will never tarnish or fade through the passing years.

You may not have a heritage such as mine, but you have the Lord, and is He not enough? Every one of us has the privilege of starting such a heritage for ourselves, our children, and our grandchildren by making sure of our own relationship with Jesus Christ.

Today in our transient society we are moving away from the meaningful concept of extended family. We don't even know our aunts, uncles, and cousins.

We as an extended family decided to try and meet now and then for a family reunion, to help close the gaps that develop when families are spread apart as we now are.

Stephan and me at home in Florida

As much as we should value the independence of our own family unit, we also should treasure the larger family, the valuable advice of parents, the care and concern of brothers and sisters and aunts and uncles, the influence of all the family members on the children. What a source of strength and support this provides, especially in times of decision or crisis. And what a source of friendship and fellowship,

diversity and unity, togetherness and individuality. That's what family is all about.

Now there are also some heated discussions when our clan gathers. It's not always peace and light and harmony. But even in those moments we have determined to disagree…agreeably. As Mother always says, "If two people agree on everything, one of them is unnecessary!"

When I look back at my own family, one of the things I'm most grateful for was their acceptance of me.

People are hungering for acceptance today in so many different ways. Clubs. Associations. Illicit sexual relationships. Even gangs. Yet God intended us to find that love and approval and acceptance within our families. We need to know that we are unconditionally loved. That doesn't mean that I have unconditional approval for everything I do, but I am loved, and I know it!

A poll was taken recently among college students and 87 percent stated a happy home as their goal. Sometimes I will listen to teenagers' conversations at the mall. One will say, "Let's go to your house." The other will answer, "Oh no, my mom doesn't want me there."

What a desolate feeling that must be!

Dr. David Goodman writes: "Every child needs to feel that his parents love, want, and enjoy him; that he matters very much to someone; and there are

Franklin's family

Anne's family

Bunny's family

Ned's family

people near who care what happens to him."

A relative of mine made a very frightening statement to my mother some time ago. He said, "If my children do not please me, I cannot love them." He used an illustration of one of his sons doing something that displeased him. The father said it was as if the boy were not his son until he came back and apologized and made things right. How unlike the love of God!

Daddy, although away from home much of the time during my formative years, commanded a deep respect. We knew that he loved us more than anything in the world, and he demonstrated this love in many open, outward expressions.

I certainly have not approved of all my children's actions. Some things have grieved Stephan and me. There have been times when I've wanted to grab some of my kids by the shoulders and shake them. But there is still unconditional love. Unconditional acceptance. I will love them for the rest of my life, and they know that.

One day years ago, when we were sitting at the table together, I asked my children what a home was to them.

My little four-year-old answered, "Mama, a home is a place where you come in out of the rain."

You know, I thought, that's it. Security. Warmth. Continuity. Protection. Reassurance.

A place to come in out of the rain....

They can face anything out in the world and come in to the warmth and shelter of home.

With the way our world is now, how deeply that shelter is needed. Outside the home, storms are fierce. We are often ignorant of all the situations our family members have to face when they are away from home: satanic spiritual pressures, school pressures, job pressures, peer pressures—just to name a few. So how much more important it is for the home to provide security.

Where else are they going to get direction?

Where else are they going to clear their heads and gain perspective?

Where are they going to catch their breath?

Where are they going to find a reference point?

A spiritual heritage builds a wall of security and protection in the home. In the Old Testament, God is often spoken of as El Shaddai, the Mother God— the all-sufficient One, protecting and providing.

I was always secure in the love of my parents, and knew that whatever I did, I would always, always be loved. Yes, it was often tough love, and never cheap sympathy, but my parents made it very clear that they always loved me, even if they didn't love what I did.

Deep down, I just knew I was loved and accepted, even when I was being punished. My parents taught us that their love was like God's love

for us: God loves a sinner, but He hates sin. My uncle used to say, "God loves us enough to accept us just the way we are, but loves us too much to leave us there." My parents felt the same way.

Daddy, although away from home much of the time during my formative years, commanded a deep respect. We knew that he loved us more than anything in the world, and he demonstrated this love in many open, outward expressions. His very presence caused me to feel shame if I had been naughty. Next to my desire to please the Lord, I wanted to please him.

I remember one day, when I was still quite young, he arrived home from a trip earlier than expected. I was in the process of doing something that I knew I shouldn't do. I can still remember how ashamed and sorry I was, and how guilty I felt as I ran down the drive and threw myself into his waiting arms. I had the assurance that he would forgive me and love me.

One paraphrase of Proverbs 31:18 says of a godly mother, "Her lamp goes not out, but it burns on continually through the night of [trouble, privation, or sorrow, warning away fear, doubt, and distrust]" (Amplified).

What a beautiful responsibility and privilege we have as mothers and wives to provide an atmosphere such as this for our loved ones.

The privileges of passing on that kind of spiritual heritage go beyond the walls of our immediate homes. Like the ripples that continue long after a stone is thrown into a quiet lake, the repercussions of a truly Christian home are widespread and persist long after the initial

Daddy snuggling with baby Antony

Mother and Daddy on their 48th wedding anniversary

influence. Aided by the gentle breeze of the Holy Spirit, the ripples lap against the shores of untold individuals, homes, and families.

In my home it started many years ago, because my ancestors decided to put Jesus first in their lives.

The ripples are continuing and growing ever larger and broader because of my family's faithfulness in passing down that godly heritage. And it will continue to grow, by the grace of God, as long as we who have received such a legacy are faithful in our personal relationship with Jesus Christ and to our God-given responsibilities in our homes.

Stop for a moment and think of how many people will be influenced by just one child raised to love the Lord Jesus, a child who has been grounded in the Word of God and has been given the living example of a godly parent or parents. The potential influence of a faithful, God-fearing parent is unending, and that staggering thought should make us revere our job, and be grateful to God that He has entrusted us with so much responsibility.

We grandchildren once asked my paternal grandmother (Mother Graham) how my grandfather and all of his family had come to know the Lord. She shyly admitted that it was because of her example.

Mother has always said that "anything that is imposed upon your children will be discarded with relief when they get old enough."

That is why I would like my children to desire the spiritual heritage that Stephan and I have attempted to pass along to them through the years from the examples they have seen.

Passing it on is a much more compelling image. Daddy is older now, but he can look on the trail behind him and see his children and grandchildren following along. Now the great-grandchildren aren't far behind!

Antony clowning on a family hike in N.C.

Lao I and Lao Niang as I remember them

4
Staying Faithful

Certainly there are days when I want to give up and throw in the towel.

But I have images of faithfulness burned into my memory, burned into my soul....

To this day I remember spending the night at my maternal grandparents' home. Waking up in the small upstairs sleeping porch, I would just lie there for a moment, listening to a thousand birds, watching the first rays of sunlight touch the ridge behind the house, savoring the fragrance of bacon, eggs, and hot biscuits drifting upstairs from Lao Niang's kitchen.

When I reached the bottom landing, I would peer around the corner into the living room.

And my grandfather, Lao I, would be there. Just as he was every morning of his life—on his knees in front of the big rocking chair. I stood watching him until Lao Niang would call us to breakfast.

69

Lao I and Lao Niang in China, early 1940s

He would get up, slowly rubbing his eyes before he replaced his glasses, his forehead still red and creased from the impact of his folded hands. Then he would see me and smile. After giving me a warm hug and a big kiss, he would wrap his arm around me, and we would walk into the kitchen together.

I knew that this active surgeon, church layman, writer, former missionary to China, and family man had been up long before dawn, spending time with the Lord. He had an extensive prayer list, and I felt warm and secure, knowing he had already prayed for me.

Lao I was one of the only Christians whom I can honestly say never disappointed me—not once. He was faithful in the little things. Though a busy doctor and writer, involved in a hundred and one things, he would kneel every morning to slip stockings on my grandmother's crippled feet and tell me it was the greatest joy of his life. He could have easily hired someone to take care of her, but he wouldn't even think of it.

I remember going through a very difficult time early in my marriage. I came back to the States from Switzerland, my emotions so used up there was almost nothing that could move me or make me cry. Almost. Two things could still bring tears into my eyes. One was thinking about Jesus Christ, and the other was watching my grandfather come into church. I know it was because of all he exemplified to me. Faithfulness. Consistency. Strength clothed in gentleness.

One of the things that encourages me most when I go back to my childhood church is seeing all the dear men and women, now gray-haired and a little frail—still faithful to the Lord, still faithful to each other. If they can remain faithful, I tell myself, then so can I.

Family prayer time at home in Montreat, N.C.

Yes, family life in these waning days of the twentieth century is uphill at best. Yes, the world wages unceasing warfare against all that we treasure and hold dear. Yes, there is immorality everywhere.

But we can remain faithful to God, because He remains faithful to us.

Lord, "I will try to walk a blameless path, but how I need Your help, especially in my own home, where I long to act as I should" (Psalm 101: 2, TLB).

One of our children defined marriage as "finding someone you want to keep." He is right. It's an unshakable commitment. You make a promise and you stick with it, come what may.

People say they want to be happy, and want to have a happy marriage. But I don't think the Bible guarantees us happiness.

In *The Gift of the Sea*, Anne Lindbergh speaks of how her friends crowded around her after she had accepted Charles Lindbergh's proposal of marriage. She recalls that they all wished her happiness.

"Don't wish me happiness," she replied to them, "but strength of character, courage, and a good sense of humor."

There was commitment in that home. That marriage was going to last no matter what. Contemporary culture has drifted far away from that sort of mindset—that deep-down heartfelt determination to make it work by God's grace.

If what I see on TV and read in women's magazines is any gauge, I'm not sure that Stephan and I have a happy marriage. The TV and radio talk shows seem to define matrimonial bliss as some kind of hormone rush or adrenaline surge. Stephan and I, however, didn't start married life as two people who blindly fell in love and were carried along on some kind of mystical chemistry.

That's just not the way it started out. It was a commitment that developed over the months and years into a deeper joy and satisfaction. Because we made that commitment to God and to each another, we have found His will, His grace, and His provision.

Men and women are turning their backs on sacred commitments today in some kind of elusive search for a happiness they will never find. They're out there…searching and searching.

Someone has well said that a man who knows one woman knows all women, but a man who knows many women knows no woman.

We were taught by word and example that marriage is a lifelong bond, not just a selfish, self-gratifying convenience. Yet if we were honest, I think all of us would admit to wondering at times if we made a mistake when we said, "I do."

Even Mrs. Billy Graham.

When Mother was first married, she lived with her parents in the beautiful mountains of North

Daddy with my two brothers, Franklin and Ned

Carolina. Daddy came up to the Chicago area and, without consulting her, accepted the pastorate of a church in Western Springs. He wrote Mother a letter and told her he had accepted this church. She was to move up, as he had already picked out the apartment…and it was "just a lovely apartment."

My prayer so often is, "Lord, even when my faith is weak or small—please keep me faithful."

She arrived a few days later, heartbroken at having to leave the mountains of North Carolina, only to find that it most certainly was not "just a lovely apartment." It was a small, dingy apartment—on the railroad tracks. Talk about depression! Mother became so despondent she put red cellophane on the wall to make it look like a fireplace and hearthside where she could sit and read. And how she hated the long cold winters of Chicago!

One day Daddy and some of his fellow workers were going into the city.

"Bill," Mother asked, "please can I just go along? I won't bother you. I just want to go window-shopping. You just leave me in Chicago on one of the streets and I'll window-shop and you can pick me up later."

Daddy said, "No. Nothing doing. This is our night out, and we're going by ourselves. Our minds are made up, and we won't take you with us."

"Oh, please. Just let me go with you!"

"No, absolutely not," and Daddy closed the door and went out.

Mother burst into tears, went in by her bed, and got on her knees. "Lord," she said, "if You'll forgive me for marrying Billy, I promise I'll never do it again!"

Now she says she'd rather have a little bit of Daddy than a whole lot of anybody else. Most of the marriages I saw growing up in Montreat were models of Ephesians 4: 32: "Be kind to one another, tenderhearted, forgiving one another, just as God in Christ forgave you" (NKJV).

Robert Quillan was right on target when he described marriage as "the union of two good forgivers."

When you decide to have that first precious baby, it's a commitment for life. I used to think it would get easier when the kids left, but once you love you are never free again. You only add more people and more commitments! There are new in-laws, grandchildren, their in-laws…life as God intended it is a progression of commitments to loved ones.

You need to make a commitment for life to each child. Children need to understand the depth of that pledge—not only the parental commitment to them but also the stability of the parents' marriage vows to each other. Since some of our good friends have divorced; my youngest son Antony becomes distressed if he even hears Stephan and me arguing.

*Stephan Nelson, reviewing the damage
immediately after Hurricane Andrew*

Basyle helping in one of Daddy's crusades

"You aren't going to get a divorce, are you?" he asks. Again and again we have reassured him that though Mom and Dad might disagree about things on occasion, we will never break our commitment to each another.

Dr. David Goodman puts it succinctly: "The best gift you can give your children," he writes, "are two parents who love each other."

So many Christians disappoint us. Yet "I live by faith in the Son of God, who loved me and gave Himself for me" (Galatians 2:20). Or as Paul reassured the Thessalonians, "The one who called you is faithful, and He will do it" (1 Thessalonians 5:24). Ultimately, it isn't even our faithfulness that counts, it is His faithfulness. The critical issue is our willingness to abide in Him, obey Him, and tap into the shoreless reservoir of His faithfulness. My prayer so often is, "Lord, even when my faith is weak or small—please keep me faithful."

I heard a Christian psychologist on the radio recently talking about dysfunctional families and their unwillingness to seek help and counsel. She said, "So many Christians seem more concerned with maintaining an image than solving a problem." Yes, Christian families are vulnerable, too!

None of us have it all together. Not even the Billy and Ruth Graham family. Not even the Stephan and Gigi Tchividjian household.

It is His faithfulness that can carry you through.

It is His faithfulness that can get you through the stormy times.

It is His faithfulness that can save and prosper our families, sometimes in spite of ourselves!

I may have been born in a godly household, but my Daddy and Mother will happily attest that I was not born with a halo. My husband could confirm that. I have in no way arrived in the Christian life. I once read that a saint is a sinner, revised and edited. Well, if that's true, I am still in the editing process. There are plenty of red marks, cross-outs, and erasures. I am a Christian, a woman, a wife, a daughter, a mother, and a friend—in progress. I do not have it all together as I write these words, nor did my family as I was growing up.

A dear friend of mine, who is a wonderful Christian wife and mother, once said that she used to go around closing all the windows before she screamed at her children. The only difference between my friend and me is that I don't bother closing the windows! Despite having Graham in my name, I am a normal daughter, wife, and mother. I often fail to live up to what I believe the Lord Jesus asks of me.

Lao I and Lao Niang in their later years. Lao I said they were the happiest years of his life.

But by His grace, and in His strength, I am still in progress.

With a husband and seven children, I have a household that never stops. Sometimes the waves of weariness and discouragement wash over me and threaten to pin me to the ground. It's not so much that I feel "unloved" or "unappreciated," it's just that every moment of my day seems claimed by someone else's needs. A verse that has given me encouragement in some of the more rugged moments is, in my paraphrase:

Come, Gigi, enter your room, and shut your doors behind you; Hide yourself, as it were, for a little moment, until the indignation is past (Isaiah 26: 20).

I can find a quiet place in the middle of the din and confusion if I remember my resources wrapped up in the person of Jesus Christ. He can bring quiet to the midst of the storm. He can give strength when I feel at the end of my own strength. He never promised to take away all the hardship or sorrow, nor untangle all the impossible situations, or remove all the giants in our lives. But He did and does promise to be with us in and through these times…and for all time.

When you are burdened by life's demands, focus your faith on God and His faithfulness, and not on your problems. Be power conscious, not problem conscious.

Former patient in China shows us the leg Lao I saved fifty years previously

Even though His strength is limitless and His faithfulness knows no bounds, there are still days when I feel utterly overcome by my human frailties. Maybe it's sweeping up all that dust that reminds me I'm only made of dust.

I remember one day when I was especially tired. I had scrubbed and cleaned and mothered since daybreak. That included tending a cranky baby who demanded ceaseless attention—and raised the roof if she felt she wasn't getting it.

I recall leaning over the bathtub in my teenage boys' room, staring at that drain…when suddenly it seemed like my life was slipping right down that drain hole. Suddenly everything caught up to me, and I felt crushed by frustration and sadness. I sat down on the floor, and the tears began to trickle down my cheek.

Lord, I remember crying, is it really worth it all?

There I was, scrubbing my life away on a bathtub that most likely no one would notice or care if it ever got scrubbed.

Then came one of those moments that are so difficult to explain. As clearly as can be, I heard a voice in my heart say, "Whatever you did for one of the least of these brothers of mine, you did for me."

A sweet quiet came over me. I realized anew that all I did out of love and commitment for my family—each necessary, meaningful task—I was also doing for Him. And more than that, He noticed every one of them. Because He was right there beside me. In that bathroom. On the floor. Beside the dirty tub.

That realization made all the difference in my attitude. I got up, dried my tears, and went back to work. For them. And for Him.

I have heard it said that discouragement is the devil's calling card.

Daddy with Stephan whom he has often referred to as one of his best friends

Stephan and me with his parents, brothers and sisters and their faithful grandmother who "prayed us together"

Daddy baptizing Jerushah

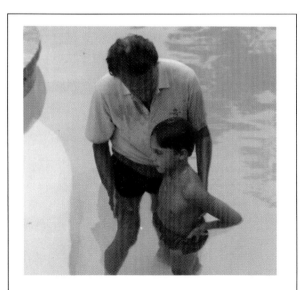

Daddy baptizing Tullian

When we are discouraged, we know that the devil has been around, and we must quickly turn our eyes away from self and return to our resource of strength.

You don't learn compassion from a book or a lecture. You learn it by experience and example. Back in Montreat, I learned compassion for others from my grandparents' example. After coming home from many busy rounds at the hospital, my grandfather would be home only five minutes before heading out the door to deliver a casserole my grandmother had made for some sick or grieving family. On Sunday afternoons, he would take me with him to visit folks in nursing homes. My grandfather helped anyone who hurt, and my grandmother cared for anyone who was sick.

Compassion and caring for others weren't things we sat around and thought about; they were just part of living. When we were children our family received monetary gifts from all over the country. Our parents used those gifts to help teach us faithfulness in giving. We started what we called a HELP fund. When some of the local people in nearby communities needed clothes or food, we went into our HELP fund and tried to make a difference in their lives.

The HELP fund was especially fun at Christmas-time. We would all sit around the kitchen table and put together packages of food and clothing and a few little toys. Then we'd go out and deliver them to nearby communities.

Those too, are images of faithfulness that are as much a part of my life as eating and sleeping.

Years ago, I wrote this prayer after reflecting on the marriage of my Grandfather and Lao Niang:

"Thank You, Lord, for the old couple.

"I have watched them all of my life. I have watched them growing old together. They have lived most of their lives, and now they are ending them together…as happy and as in love as when they first began.

My grandfather helped anyone who hurt, and my grandmother cared for anyone who was sick.

"Thank You, Lord, for allowing me the privilege of living near them, for allowing me the moments I have shared with them, for allowing me to share in their love.

"Thank You, Lord…for letting me see them holding hands in the car as they drive along the freeway…for the times I've seen him bend over her pain-ridden body, look into her eyes, kiss her gently on the lips like a young lover and say, 'How is my sweetheart today?'

"Thank You for the example they are to young lovers, for the way he gently cares for her in her pain even though he himself is not well. Thank You for the way he understands her needs without a spoken word, for how sweetly he reacts with

Bunny, Anne, Mother and I visit Mother's birthplace...China

tenderness or a joke when, because of her pain, she becomes cross.

"Thank You for her, for her devotion and love for him. For the faithful way she has followed and cared for him even when times were difficult. For their sweet oneness that makes it so she will allow no other person to care for her.

"But most of all, thank You for their love and devotion to You. Thank You for allowing me to be their granddaughter.

"Through them, I have seen real love."

Abiding in the person of Jesus Christ is an everyday, moment-by-moment growing process. We abide by saturating ourselves with the Word of God. Each of us needs a special time each day to let God speak to us through His Word. I went to a Christian high school in Florida which taught, "No Bible, no breakfast"—encouraging the habit of early morning devotions. And I still believe it is crucial to teach good habits.

For some, the early morning hours are best. My Mother always got up before we children did to have time with the Lord. I've tried that...but somehow I find the pressures of the day beginning to crowd in on me as soon as I open my eyes. Since I tend to be a night person anyway, I prefer my time with the Lord at the close of the day, after the kids are asleep, when the house is relatively clean, and all is quiet.

The "when" isn't the important thing.

The important thing is time alone with the Lord who loves you.

In our house growing up, family devotions weren't something long and drawn out. It was just a simple Bible reading, a simple prayer.

At the Tchividjian home, we try to turn our family's attention to the Lord for a few moments after supper. Invariably, the phone rings, the dog starts barking, or someone bangs on the front door.

In our house growing up, family devotions weren't something long and drawn out. It was just a simple Bible reading, a simple prayer.

But the principle that comes across to my children is that reading the Scriptures and praying is important enough to Mommy and Daddy to keep on trying. Even with all the interruptions. Even with all the failures and minor disasters. Even though it's never been easy.

Our now grown and married son, Stephan Nelson, once said, "You know Mom, those devotions of ours sort of capsulize the Christian life."

"How's that?" I asked him.

"Well," he laughed, "you get discouraged, things go

81

wrong, and you want to give up. But you keep doing it."

Seeing my grown children now encountering the same obstacles, yet persevering in their family devotions makes all those nerve-jangling interruptions seem worthwhile.

Prayer is simply talking to God.

As soon as I could talk, I was taught to pray out loud, and before I could talk, I was taught by example to pray about everything and anything. Nothing was too big or too small to speak to God about. I discovered very early the joys of answered prayer, and have continued to rejoice as I become more and more conscious of the heights yet to be scaled in my prayer life.

Our soul's greatest need is communion with God, and prayer fulfills a great part of this need.

Stephan's mother (now past 90) with Jerushah in Switzerland

We have a rather large yard for southern Florida and, since we have a twelve-month growing season, we seem to spend endless hours working in it. My sons often balk at another Saturday doing yard work, so I repeatedly point out to them that God's mandate to subdue the land existed before the Fall of Man and was considered a privilege for Adam. Even this biblical encouragement doesn't seem to have much effect on their attitudes.

One day as we were "subduing" vines and leaves, our fourth son Aram, whose job it was to pick up leaves, just kept plopping from leaf pile to leaf pile, all the while singing at the top of his eight-year-old lungs, "Work, work, I hate work. It's so dumb and dull."

I have to admit he had a point, but someone has to do it. Twice a year, we have to fertilize our lawn. We usually choose a fertilizer that is supposed to kill the weeds and feed the grass. However, we always do this with fear and trepidation, since the weeds outnumber the grass. What if we awaken one morning to a dead yard?

One year as we were repeating the weeding and feeding process, it occurred to me that this is the ministry of the Holy Spirit in our lives.

From the day we first trust Christ, He begins to weed out the unhealthy, negative desires that influence us and replace them with wholesome desires for spiritual, mental, and moral well-being.

He is the Gardener. But I wonder…does He just kick His way in through the garden gate of our lives and begin whacking away at the weeds and vines…or does He wait for an invitation? Does He force-feed us His truth, or wait until our heart is ready soil to receive it?

We have a faithful Gardener who waits at the garden gate each morning, tools ready, sleeves rolled up. How often do we leave Him standing at the gate

Mother still looking adoringly at her sweetheart of 50 years

all day? How faithful are we to meet Him, humbly open our lives, and let Him do His work?

Faithfulness is simply persevering. It is falling down and getting up again. It is washing the same socks for the ten-thousandth time. It is saying "I forgive you" and "I'm sorry, would you please forgive me?" over and over and over again—and meaning it.

The apostle Paul described the Christian life as pressing toward the goal (see Philippians 3:14). That's perseverance.

Mother Teresa describes holiness as "doing God's will with a smile." That's perseverance.

I think of my mother, being left at home again and again, out of the spotlight, shunning the glory. And she is such a capable woman. She probably has more knowledge of Scripture than Daddy. She could probably prepare a better sermon than Daddy. Yet she has willingly directed her focus and energies to keeping the flowers blooming, the hearth warm, the dishes clean, and five independent-minded children fed and clothed and pointed toward service for Jesus Christ.

That, my friends, is perseverance, too.

If you are as faithful as you know how to be in your calling as a spouse or a parent, and yet suffer burdens, grief, and disappointments, I have a word of encouragement for you. I firmly believe it will be God's greatest pleasure to spend all eternity making this up to you.

In Matthew 19:29, Jesus spoke tenderly to the

Stephan Nelson

*My two eldest children helping in
one of Daddy's crusades*

Berdjette

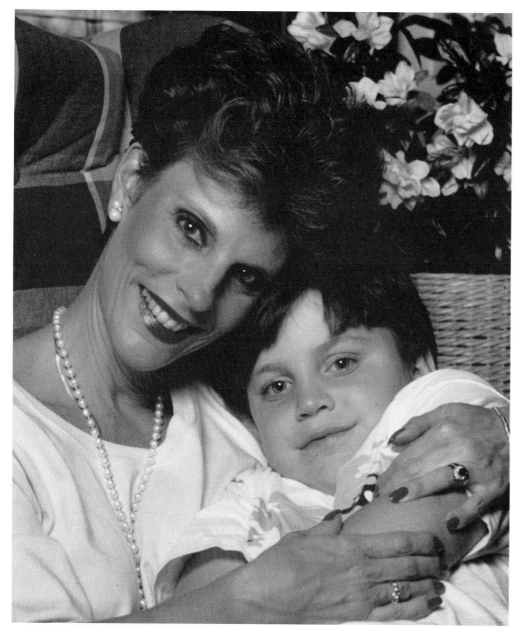

Antony and me

disciples who had endured hardship and personal sacrifice to follow Him so faithfully through the years of His earthly ministry. He assured them that the family traumas they had endured for the sake of His name would not go unremembered in eternity.

In his letter to the Ephesians, Paul took out his sketchpad and penciled one of the most glorious glimpses of God's eternal design in all of Scripture. As you study this awesome vision of the future with the eyes of your heart, you will see hints and glimpses of our Father's future plans for His children. Paul writes:

"Because of his great love for us, God, who is rich in mercy, made us alive with Christ even when we were dead in transgressions—it is by grace you have been saved. And God raised us up with Christ and seated us with him in the heavenly realms in Christ Jesus, in order that in the coming ages he might show the incomparable riches of his grace, expressed in his kindness to us in Christ Jesus" (Ephesians 2: 4-7).

In the book of Revelation, the Lord Jesus encourages the believers in Smyrna to "be faithful, even to the point of death, and I will give you the crown of life" (2: 10).

No one knows what that "crown of life"—that ultimate reward for faithfulness—looks like, or feels like, or means. We can only be sure that if it is a crown given by the King of Kings…it is worth having. No matter what.

A recent family photograph: left to right, me, Anne, Bunny, Mother, Daddy, Franklin and Ned

EPILOGUE

Beginning Now

Today if you hear his voice, do not harden your hearts (Hebrews 3: 7).

Behold, now is the accepted time; behold, now is the day of salvation (2 Corinthians 6: 2, NKJV).

Seek the LORD while he may be found; call on him while he is near. Let the wicked forsake his way and the evil man his thoughts. Let him turn to the LORD, and he will have mercy on him, and to our God, for he will freely pardon (Isaiah 55: 7).

Sow for yourselves righteousness; Reap in mercy; Break up your fallow ground, For it is time to seek the LORD, Till He comes and rains righteousness on you (Hosea 10: 12, NKJV).

On the last and greatest day of the Feast, Jesus stood and said in a loud voice, "If anyone is thirsty, let him come to me and drink. Whoever believes in me, as the Scripture has said, streams of living water will flow from within him" (John 7: 37-38).

My son Aram's high school
senior picture 1993

My daughter Jerushah

Some of you are at a place in your life where a fresh start would be perfectly timed.

Your children are still young and impressionable. Your marriage is still finding its way and developing patterns and habits. You have time to pick up your spiritual heritage and develop it, or begin a new one.

Others of you may be thinking, I've blown too many opportunities. I've made too many mistakes. I've wasted too many years. I've turned down too many wrong side trails and hit too many dead ends. It's too late for me to begin a spiritual heritage.

That just isn't true! Yes, our sinful actions or neglect has consequences. And no, we can't go back and do things over again. But it is never too late to begin passing on a spiritual heritage. The painter Andrew Wyeth once said that an artist's greatest irritation is having his work criticized before it is finished. If you are alive and reading these words, God is not finished with you.

As you have looked at the pictures in this book and read through the text, you may have found yourself thinking, Well, I certainly didn't have the kind of heritage that Gigi did. And I haven't been faithful in my responsibilities. I haven't been a faithful Christian, a faithful spouse, a faithful parent. I've failed so often.

How I love those gracious words of the psalmist,

"If you, O LORD, kept a record of sins,
O Lord, who could stand?
But with you there is forgiveness;
therefore you are feared"
(Psalm 130: 3-4).

How could any of us stand before the Lord or try to serve Him if He were not a gracious, forgiving God? There is forgiveness with Him! There is forgiveness in His Son!

Listen to the words of Paul:

"In face of all this, what is there left to say? If God is for us, who can be against us? He who did not grudge his own Son but gave him up for us all—can we not trust such a God to give us, with him, everything else we need?

My son Tullian wearing earrings, a gift from "Tai Tai," my children's name for my Mother

Left to right: Jerushah, David, Berdjette, Stephan, Lydia, Basyle, me,
Lisa, Stephan Nelson, Aram, Tullian, Stetson waving, Antony

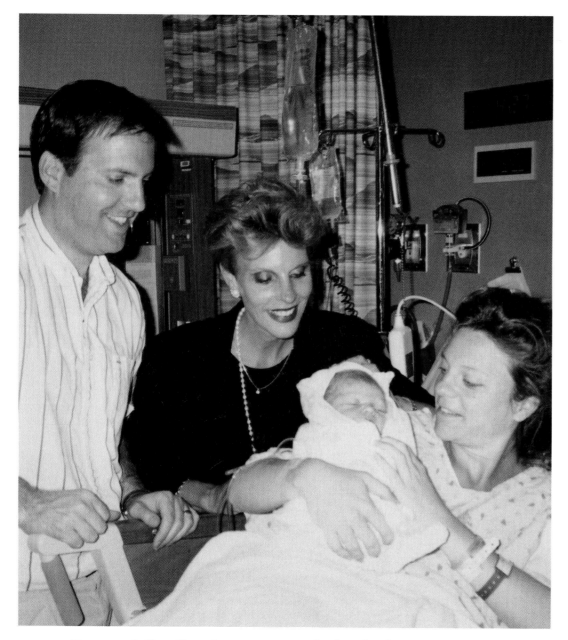

I was privileged to be present at the birth of my grandson, Seth Barker, 1992

"Who would dare accuse us, whom God has chosen? The judge himself has declared us free from sin. Who is in a position to condemn? Only Christ, and Christ died for us, Christ rose for us, Christ reigns in power for us, Christ prays for us!" (Romans 8: 33-34, Phillips).

It is our Lord God who is faithful. And He invites us as stumbling, imperfect, often failing husbands and wives and mothers and fathers and sons and daughters to discover His forgiveness and wrap our lives in His wonderful faithfulness.

It doesn't depend on your human heritage! With His help, you can begin a habit and pattern of faithfulness from this moment on!

Feel free to walk through the gate anytime. It is always open.

Every family heritage of faithfulness must begin with someone. Perhaps, at this very moment, it could begin with you.

As you have looked through the pages of this book, I pray that you have seen not so much the pictures of a famous family, but the big picture of a faithful God. I pray also that you have sensed an invitation not only into our hearts and home, but into a personal relationship with our Lord and Saviour Jesus Christ.

Perhaps you have felt a growing desire to seek God…but you're not sure where to start. Good news! He is already seeking you!

He stands at the door of your home. He stands at the door of your life.

"Behold, I stand at the door and knock; if anyone hears my voice and opens the door, I will come in to him, and will dine with him, and he with Me." (Revelation 3: 20)

All you have to do is open the door.

Come back anytime

A PERSONAL WORD

Many families are hurting today and Christians are not exempt.

I personally have suffered two bouts with clinical depression. We have had a teenage son run away from home, and we have suffered with a family member as she dealt with the agony of divorce.

Because of these and other difficulties our family has experienced, and because of my husband Stephan's profession as a clinical psychologist, I have a tender heart for all who are hurting. For this reason, I became the national women's advisor for Rapha Hospitals.

Rapha—which in Hebrew means "the God who heals"—is an organization with treatment centers in hospitals across the country. Our experience has shown that Rapha programs offer a unique blend of clinical competence and biblical truth that can lead to emotional and spiritual healing.

Does someone in your family suffer from depression, an eating disorder, substance abuse, suicidal tendencies or other emotional problems? Is there a "prodigal," a runaway teen, an unwed pregnant daughter, an abusive mate in your family?

I would not hesitate to trust one of my family members to Rapha. If you or someone close to you has emotional problems, maybe we can be of help, just call me—1-800-383-HOPE

Sincerely,